Table of Contents:

Introduction

Confusion. Loneliness. Addiction. We need not speak of their impact on the human heart and their common occurrence in modern society. Those who live with these symptoms of our fallen world know enough. With such inner trials, though, what hope is there of healing and recovery, a sense of joy and peace? For those who have tasted the sweetness of God's Presence in their prayer, the hope is alive and real. If you have tasted this sweetness, I hope this book will help to deepen your relationship with God, as you continue through your trials on your journey to Heaven. And for those who have not and who do not pray? I hope this book will help you to take the first step in finding the unconditional love of God in prayer. But in order to truly grasp the value and meaning of prayer, we must first ask: what is prayer?

The most common definition of prayer seems to be "communication with God", but this doesn't get to the heart of the matter. Prayer goes to the very core of our being. It goes to the very center of who we are and who God is. Communication, on the other hand, is done externally, with words, spoken and heard, and with body language. Prayer goes much deeper than our words and is the realization of a union with God in the silent space of our hearts.

True, what I have written is a book of words. Yet the purpose is not to come up with a precise definition of prayer or to teach specific methods of prayer. Instead, the purpose is twofold. First, to encourage you to be open to experience God's Presence in prayer, and second, to encourage you to stay close to Him in prayer throughout your life's journey.

Each section of the book is comprised of scripture[1], reflections, and a brief tale. It is ultimately through the Word of God that our journey of prayer takes place - the Word of Love written in our hearts. It is my hope that these words will help you

---

[1] All translations are taken from the New American Bible Revised Edition.

to reach those depths in your heart so that you may come to know how fully you are loved by God.

Part One:
God is Love

Prayer is a tree growing silently, slowly day and night. It does not move about but stays rooted. It waits patiently and expectantly for sun and rain, wind and snow. It looks toward the skies and opens its leaves to all.

Let us begin our journey by dwelling on a passage from the first letter of John, where we are reminded of the greatness and the method of God's love for us. John tells us[2], "In this way the love of God was revealed to us: God sent his only Son into the world so that we might have life through him. In this is love: not that we have loved God, but that he loved us and sent his Son as expiation for our sins." Notice that John's evidence of God's love is to be found in the person of His Son, and particularly, in His Son's mission. When we encounter Jesus, we encounter God's love, and when we encounter God's love, we find life. And what is life? Again, we can turn to John for an answer. In the wonderful prologue to His Gospel[3], he states, "All things came to be through him, and without him nothing came to be. What came to be through him was life, and this life was the light of the human race." John equates life with light, and implies that Jesus is the light of the world. As he continues in his prologue[4], "The light shines in the darkness, and the darkness has not overcome it." Jesus is the light that shines in the darkness. Jesus is life. Therefore, when we encounter Jesus in prayer, we encounter life itself. It is only in Him that we find who we are meant to be. It is only in His love for us that we radiate His light, breathe in His life, and fulfill our selves.

Never, never, never doubt the immensity of God's love for you. It is perhaps the single greatest error that we can make in our spiritual lives because, when we doubt His love for us, we become terribly confused, lost, and we wander spiritually. It is then that we lose our light and our life. At the moment when we lose sight of His love, we simultaneously lose sight of our very selves. That is why, like a tree, we must stay rooted in God's love, that is, rooted in prayer. It is only in this way that we can grow.

Now we are ready to answer the menacingly simple question: why follow Christ? The answer: He desires what is best

---

[2] 1 John 4:9-10
[3] John 1:3-4
[4] John 1:5

for you and is leading you on the path to attain it. But perhaps you see the suffering in the world and have doubts. Perhaps you see the suffering that you've experienced on your own journey and you doubt His love. But look at Jesus on the cross. Do you see His love for you there? Do you see Him smiling at you? He is joyful on the cross because, in His heart, you are worth the price He paid. As Paul says in his letter to the Romans[5] "God proves his love for us in that while we were still sinners Christ died for us."

It is true that the evil of the world is dark, but remember that it can only be dark when compared with light, and it can only be evil when compared with goodness. When we are disturbed by the darkness of suffering and doubts, is it not because we have known joy and peace? Is there not also love in the world? Have faith then, and persevere in your prayer, for darkness can only be seen by the light of goodness. Therefore, God is in your heart, and you have met Him. He is the source of all that is beautiful, true, and good that you have experienced. He can and will restore you to the fullness of life if you but remain in His healing embrace.

Perhaps now you can see the bud of beauty in this world that is ready to blossom in the land of Eternal Spring. Hang on to what is good and beautiful in the world, hang on to Jesus in your heart, and you will see that God is showing you the path to life. Trust in His plan, and have faith in the One whom you know to be love. But what about God's justice? Won't God punish us when we turn away from our sinfulness to face Him?

A beautiful insight was made by Martin Luther King, Jr. when he said[6], "justice is love correcting that which revolts against love." In other words, the purpose of justice is not punishment. Rather, the purpose of justice is to change the heart of the person. When the heart of the person is oriented towards God it will find Divine Mercy. The point of justice is to bring God's presence into the heart of the sinner along with the peace that comes with it. His

---

[5] Romans 5:8
[6] King Jr., Martin Luther. "Address to 1st Montgomery Improvement Association." Holt Street Baptist Church. Montgomery, AL. 5 December 1955.

justice is always for our flourishing and fulfillment as human beings. Its purpose is to lead us to Him and drive out those things which cause destruction in our lives. We must know at all times that God is love and that His ultimate aim is to share His joy with us. The end of His justice, is our joy.

Consider that, when speaking of how He will save Israel from the false shepherds who would spiritually destroy His flock, God says through His prophet Ezekiel[7],

> In good pastures I will pasture them; on the mountain heights of Israel will be their grazing land. There they will lie down on good grazing ground; in rich pastures they will be pastured on the mountains of Israel. I myself will pasture my sheep; I myself will give them rest—oracle of the Lord God. The lost I will search out, the strays I will bring back, the injured I will bind up, and the sick I will heal; but the sleek and the strong I will destroy. I will shepherd them in judgment.

It is necessary for God to be the meek and gentle Shepherd as well as the Lord of Hosts with wrath of fire. He is meek and gentle to His sheep that listen to His voice and that are led to the fullness of life, yet His wrath blazes against the false shepherds and the wolves that would devour them along the way. He must protect His sheep. That is why He is necessarily just and merciful at the same time.

Everything good in our life flows from God, and His presence is discovered in the silence of our prayer. It is He who leads us in truth and in love to the fulfillment of our person. So, we must be attentive to His voice. He will not lead us astray, nor abandon us. Again, look to the cross. He desires our happiness with all His heart. He is worthy of the worship of our whole heart because He is love, and He wills our joy. As Jesus says in John's Gospel[8], "I came so that they might have life, and have it more abundantly. I am the good shepherd. A good shepherd lays down

---

[7] Ezekiel 34:14-16
[8] John 10:10b-11

his life for the sheep." We can and should become used to the feel of the Good Shepherd by spending time in His restful presence. We can turn over all our concerns to Him by placing our hearts in His gentle hands, wounded for us. Just as sheep will recognize their shepherd, we will begin to recognize the ways in which God is working in our lives and leading us to greener pastures. Then, we can discern more clearly between the false shepherds who would use us for their own gains and the Good Shepherd who wants only what is best for us.

Further, consider Psalm 136, where the constant refrain is, "His mercy endures forever." The psalmist goes through the history of Israel, from the formation of the world, through the wandering in the wilderness of the desert, and to the arrival at the promised land, all the while proclaiming, "His mercy endures forever." The psalmist sees God's mercy in all the aspects of Israel's journey, both good and bad. He has faith that everything works towards God's ultimate end, which is our life.

Just as the Israelites had to rely on the mercy of the Lord to free them from slavery and bring them to the Promised Land, so we must place ourselves in the hands of our Heavenly Father in order to find our true life. We must recognize that we are small and needy and that God is big and loving. Indeed, we will realize just how small we are and just how big God is when we place our hearts into His infinitely compassionate hands.

As we deepen our realization of this truth, we will see that love is His only motivation. Everything He does in our lives is for our spiritual well-being. Those seemingly negative attributes of God, such as wrath, if taken as His base motivations for His actions, make God look small in love. But we know that this is the opposite of the truth. He is boundless love. We must see this, lest we get the wrong picture of God and turn away from Him in despair. God is love, and we must allow Him to love us in the silence of our hearts. Only then we will begin to understand how big God is, and that His mercy is bigger than any of our sins.

✳✳✳

Deep Forest

There was once a renowned hermit who was famous for never speaking a word. He stayed in one spot day and night, listening. No one knew how long he had been there, but everyone agreed it was longer than they had been alive. I had a desire that burned in my heart for a long time, and finally I found the courage to go to him. I was sure he would help.

He sat there, Indian-style, with closed eyes, at the edge of a great forest. I approached him and said, "I want to know God, can you help me?" He took a deep breath, opened his eyes, exhaled, and closed them again.

I wasn't sure that he heard me so I said to him again, "I want to know God, can you help me?" Again, he did the same thing, opened his eyes, breathed deeply, and closed them again. I still didn't understand, so I said to him a third time, "Please help me! I want to know God!"

For the third time, he opened his eyes and closed them again with a deep breath. Finally, I understood. I entered right into that deep forest, and I never came back.

Prayer is a flower, small and beautiful, speaking only with its grace.
It springs from ordinary places and adds its extraordinary elegance.

In the first chapter, we reflected on Jesus' mission and how His crucifixion reveals His love for us. There is other evidence, however, of God's love. We are surrounded by it. God, and His love, are reflected in the beauty of His creation. We can almost hear Azariah and his companions proclaiming through the blazing furnace[9], "Let the earth bless the Lord, praise and exalt him above all forever." Just take a second to contemplate the things around you and how intricately beautiful they are at this moment.

Imagine the color of the sky during a spring sunset. Can you see in your mind's eye the color of pale yellow fading into deep blue, where grey clouds dash in airy lengths? Can you see the black blots of trees standing tall against the sky? Imagine brushing your hands along grass beneath you. Feel the cool breath of air that gently caresses your cheeks. Hear the crickets chirping. Watch the birds flutter along their path to find shelter for the night. Smell the briskness of dusk. Do you see the evening star poking its shy head out of the darkness?

Now turn again to the moment that is upon you. Take it in, more than words can express. Breathe deeply, and smell the air. Feel the wonderful textures on your skin. Soak in the peace, the meaning, and the magnificence. All of this was given to you by God. Why? Because He loves you. He loves your existence, and gives this moment to you. The goodness and beauty of creation is nothing less than God pouring out His love upon us. Each flower, cloud, and ray of sun portrays His love for us and His joy in our existence. It is in this moment of being that we experience the Presence of God.

Consider the book of Genesis, which begins with the fantastic event of creation, where God, displaying the immensity of his power[10], "created the heavens and the earth— and the earth was without form or shape, with darkness over the abyss and a mighty wind sweeping over the waters." Does this not display His great love? Is not the event of creation dripping with it? God

---

[9] Daniel 3:74
[10] Genesis 1:1-2

continues His work by saying[11], "Let us make human beings in our image, after our likeness. Let them have dominion over the fish of the sea, the birds of the air, the tame animals, all the wild animals, and all the creatures that crawl on the earth." The author concludes this section by stating[12], "God looked at everything he had made, and found it very good." Why did God, who is the source of life, the source of love, and the source of joy find it very good? It is because He poured His life, His love, and His joy into His creation, and particularly, He poured them into us, for[13], "God created mankind in his image; in the image of God he created them." The author of Genesis purposefully repeats the phrase to emphasize its importance.

The variety and beauty of creation is simply astounding, especially when we consider that God created color out of the complete absence of color – even the darkness of an abyss. He created sound out of the absence of all sounds – including silence. All of creation is unprecedented and could not have been fathomed by any of us. He created minds and bodies and joined them together in the most exciting way. God created the waters to envelop us like clothes when we plunge into them. He created them to fall out of the sky as gentle as flowers and as white as doves. From the distant stars, to the specks of dust, and from the soaring birds to the marching ants, all of this says, "I love you." All of this comprises our home. It is beautiful, humorous, inspiring, and fascinating - especially to those who can still marvel at creation as when they were children discovering it for the first time. It is here that we can meet God in prayer, reflected as an artist in His work.

However, do not think that God is distant; He is right here in your heartbeat. Do not search for Him among the stars, or if you do, search for Him in their appearance to your eye and in the wonder that they stir in your heart. God is all around you and

---

[11] Genesis 1:26
[12] Genesis 1:31
[13] Genesis 1:27

right inside of you, at the very center of your being, holding all creation in His hands. He is with you wherever you go.

The psalmist proclaims to God[14], "you have given my heart more joy than they have when grain and wine abound." It is God's creation that has made his spirit drunk with the joy of His presence. The purity of God's smile shines upon all of our souls like the smile of a newborn child. It is pure and loving, not forced and not demanding, always bringing joy. His smile never fades and never wearies of shining upon you, just as the sunshine never wearies of bringing its rays upon the flowers of earth.

As we continue to reflect on these truths, we realize that we can take our contemplative prayer life with us as we go about our days as a Presence in our heart that we can turn to. He is sustaining us at all times. He is the reason and source of our being. His loving presence is our peace. As Jesus tells His apostles on the eve of His Passion, when darkness was on the horizon for all of them[15], "I will ask the Father, and he will give you another Advocate to be with you always, the Spirit of truth, which the world cannot accept, because it neither sees nor knows it. But you know it, because it remains with you, and will be in you. I will not leave you orphans; I will come to you." At any moment in our day, we can turn our inner gaze to Him, if only for a second. Thus, we can welcome Him into every aspect of our lives, and carry our contemplative life into our everyday life, His presence reflected in the beauty of what surrounds us.

God's grace is found in this moment. He is right here, right now, and it is in this time that we can be with Him. Since it is only He that can give our hearts peace, we find our peace with Him in the present. Since He is love, it is in the present that we can find the love we are looking for. As the psalmist proclaims[16], "You are my shelter; you guard me from distress; with joyful shouts of

---

[14] Psalm 4:8
[15] John 14:16-18
[16] Psalm 32:7

deliverance you surround me." He surrounds us with His loving presence, patiently waiting for us to turn to Him in our hearts.

We will cultivate gratitude by recognizing all the good things in our lives as flowing from God's love for us. We will recognize Him as the source of all that is good, beautiful, and true in our lives. Our very life comes from Him, and He calls us His children. Life is a precious gift, and we find its fullness in prayer.

Sister Rain

As I was walking through the fields one day, I came across the most beautiful flowers. They were full of vibrant colors and rich aromas. I asked them how they became so beautiful, and they replied that it was because Brother Sun was shining on them so often. But they continued to say that Sister Rain was hurtful to them, and that they would be even more beautiful without her. They said that she made them cold and lonely for no one would come to see their beauty out in the rain. They asked me if I could reason with Sister Rain to stop visiting them.

So, I climbed up the mountains and into the clouds to talk to Sister Rain and told her how she was hurting the flowers. But she only giggled. "I'm not hurting them," she said, "They need me to become so beautiful. It may seem to them that I am hurtful and I am sorry for that, but without me they would perish. Just ask Brother Sun."

When I asked Brother Sun he said the same, "There is a balance between sister and I that brings about their beauty. They need us both." So, I went down the mountain and told the flowers what Brother Sun and Sister Rain had said. And would you believe it? They have come to welcome Sister Rain.

Prayer is a speck of dust floating in the sunlight, gentle, soft, and unnoticeable to those who are in a rush.

In the first two chapters, we looked at two different ways that God reveals His love for us. Specifically, at the end of the first chapter, we mentioned how God is "big", and we are "small". We will now examine this a little closer. In a sense, it is more accurate to say that we are nothing, and this statement is frequently used in spiritual writings. What does it mean to say this? Certainly, we must not take it literally, for we share in God's Being. Rather, it is to say that, without God, we cannot exist, because He is the source of all existence - He is Being-itself.

But what is Being-itself? This is a question that philosophers have pondered for thousands of years without coming to a definitive answer. There is always something mysterious about Being, something that we cannot penetrate with our minds, yet something that is familiar to us, because we share in it. We aren't going to get into an in-depth discussion of this topic, but an overview helps us to better understand who we are and our relationship with God.

Again, let us state, God is Being, and we cannot exist without Him for He is the foundation of all existence. He is the source of all life; He is life. Without our participation in Being (that is to say God), we would be no-thing. It is in this sense that we say we are nothing - our being is entirely dependent on God.

From all of this it follows that, the more we enter into the life of God, the more we find life-itself. The more we enter into He-Who-Is, the more we fulfill our selves. This is what prayer recognizes and accomplishes. When we pray, we are admitting the truth of our nothingness and God's "everything-ness". We are recognizing that we only reach our full stature as persons, when we find ourselves in God. God is leading us towards Himself, but He is also leading us towards our fullest selves. In prayer, we grow into the person that God wants us to be - we mature into our spiritual selves, just as a child matures into an adult. Even though we are like a piece of dust when compared to the almighty presence of God, it is God who, in His love, stoops down and breathes life into us.[17]

Yet, this transformation does not happen overnight. Oftentimes, God is silent in our prayer, and His work in our souls goes unnoticed. He works secretly in the depths of our hearts where we cannot observe the tender care that He is giving our souls from one moment to the next, bringing about His will and His work in our lives. God speaks to us through Isaiah the prophet saying[18], "my thoughts are not your thoughts, nor are your ways my ways—oracle of the Lord. For as the heavens are higher than the earth, so are my ways higher than your ways, my thoughts higher than your thoughts." Still, at times we shall be able to reflect and see how far we have come without knowing how. Even though we feel like we are treading water in the silence of our prayer, God is still bringing us, without our knowing how, closer to Himself. God continues speaking through His prophet[19], "So shall my word be that goes forth from my mouth; It shall not return to me empty, but shall do what pleases me, achieving the end for which I sent it."

We can now see that the two keys of prayer are this: first that we open our hearts to the loving gaze of our Heavenly Father, especially those areas where we are hurting or rebellious, and second, that we rest in His presence. It is through our prayer that we come to know our freedom and identity as God's beloved children. St. Paul reminds us in his letter to the Galatians[20], "As proof that you are children, God sent the spirit of his Son into our hearts, crying out, 'Abba, Father!' So, you are no longer a slave but a child, and if a child then also an heir, through God."

However, sometimes in our prayer, we can get into the habit of talking to God or thinking about God, as if He were distant, almost imaginary. Because we do not physically see and hear Him, it is difficult to remember that He is right there, present with us, listening to us and breathing His life into us. It is good to keep this

---

[17] Genesis 2:7
[18] Isaiah 55:8-9
[19] Isaiah 55:11
[20] Galatians 4:6-7

in the forefront of our minds as we pray so that our being-with-Him remains a living and intimate connection. Remember that He is truly present, listening to your heart and speaking to you there.

We must remember that God is always right here in our hearts, always accessible, always offering Himself to us. Even in the midst of the busyness of our lives we can turn to Him in short breaths of prayer. Even though our body may be busy, our soul can be as though it were far away on a mountain top, drifting in a breeze, watching the distant trees sway and the clouds float by, completely at peace, resting in Him. This is possible because there is a part of us that is unchanging - the center of our being, where God is sustaining us. It is our soul, the meeting place with God.

Here, in this spot, we are vulnerable, but here also, we are loved. Again, we turn to Isaiah[21], "Do not fear, for I have redeemed you; I have called you by name: you are mine." It is good for us to give our hearts to Christ throughout our days. When we are at work, at play, or at home, we can take brief moments to place our hearts into the wounded hands of Christ. Our hearts may be sorrowful, distressed, sinful, anxious, restless, frustrated, joyful, prayerful, or in any state. It does not matter. What matters is that we offer it to Him in trust and stay present to Him. He keeps us grounded and helps to prevent wounds from being created or deepened. He gives us guidance. He shares our joys and pains and gives us grace. He is there for us in all things. It is very important for us to keep our hearts in His hands.

There are many good short prayers, including scripture quotes, that one can repeat in order to keep aflame their contemplative mind. One such example is, "Lord, I offer this moment to be with you." Anything that keeps us aware of the Lord's presence and our need for Him is good. We have so little to offer Him in response to His great love for us, yet He doesn't ask great things of us. All He asks is that we open our hearts to Him in this moment, and let Him guide us to the fulness of life. As Jesus reminds us through John's Gospel[22],

---

[21] Isaiah 43:1

Remain in me, as I remain in you. Just as a branch cannot
bear fruit on its own unless it remains on the vine, so
neither can you unless you remain in me. I am the vine, you
are the branches. Whoever remains in me and I in him will
bear much fruit, because without me you can do nothing.
In each moment, we can offer Him an open heart through which
His love can flow. It is this gift which He desires with great
intensity – the gift of our open hearts.

✳✳✳

The Secret

Rumors swirled about a hermit who knew the secret of
prayer. Well, as you can imagine, I wanted to know the secret too,
so I inquired about where he could be found. I was told that he
lived at the top of a mountain which could only be reached by
climbing a steep cliff, but no one dared climb it. I was a pretty
good climber, and I was even more impatient, so I climbed it the
next day.

When I got to the top there was no one there. I waited for a
week, and still no one showed up. After that I resigned myself to
failure and climbed back down. When I reached the bottom, I lay
in the grass and stared at the clouds hanging in the sky, wondering
about the secret.

As I lay there I began to shrink, and I continued to shrink
and to shrink. Eventually, I shrank so small that I found myself
floating on a piece of dust. I heard a voice inquire, "So, you want to
know the secret of prayer?" Lo and behold, it was he who knew!

---

[22] John 15:4-5

I noted that he was floating on dust too, and I said, "Yes, please tell me."

He replied with one word – "little".

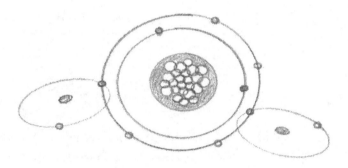

Prayer is a field of tall grass waving in the wind. Its crests and troughs provide a rhythm and meaning to life.

We focused in the previous chapter on bringing our contemplative life into our everyday life. Now, we will examine the effects of prayer in more detail. It is God who gives meaning to our existence. When He enters our life, we find that meaning is restored. Where once we were lost and confused, now we have direction and purpose. This is because when we draw close to God, He breathes into us the life of our fullest self, and as we become our fullest self, we find our meaning in God's family.

Our meaning is deeply connected with our relationships with others and our relationship with God. When we discover our fullest self, we also discover the gifts which God has endowed us with. It is these gifts that we, in turn, develop and use for others. We draw close to God in prayer, God gives us the gift of ourselves, and we then give the gift of ourselves to our brothers and sisters in God's family[23]. These gifts can be spiritual, intellectual, artistic, relational, and more. In this giving, we come to discover our true meaning, which is bound up in our relationships with God and with others.

Relationships are not only a giving but also a receiving. Consider the Trinity, where there is a constant flow of love from one Person to the Other. They give and receive each Other's love and life. Therefore, we exist not only to give, but also to receive. We give ourselves to others, and we receive their gifts to us, just as we received the gift of ourselves from God. As we read in Matthew's Gospel[24], "your light must shine before others, that they may see your good deeds and glorify your heavenly Father." This giving and receiving furthers our joy and sense of fulfillment. Remember from our first chapter that John equates light with life. We are meant to spread life to others through the gifts that God has given us. Our gifts are like the wind that blows waves of joy through the field of life.

Consider the Word of God spoken through the prophet Jeremiah[25], "Before I formed you in the womb I knew you, before

---

[23] 1 Corinthians 12:12
[24] Matthew 5:16

In Loving Memory of
Richard Nicholas
Schneider

Born: November 10, 1955
Died: August 5, 2016

Remember me when flowers bloom
Early in the spring
Remember me on sunny days
In the fun that summer brings

Remember me in the fall
As you walk through
the leaves of gold
And in the wintertime remember me
In stories that are told

But most of all remember
Each day right from the start
I will be forever near
For I live within your heart

you were born I dedicated you, a prophet to the nations I appointed you." God chose for you to exist. He chose to create you because He loved you even before you existed. He saw who you would be, the gifts that you would bring to the world, and He loved you. He also died for you, that you might become the fullness of yourself, your happiest self, all out of love for you. He calls you by name and says, "Together, we can do this, you and me." You can count on His grace and His presence. He thinks highly of you, and He is calling you into a deep and life-changing relationship with Himself. Do not be afraid to unite your life to His and to use your gifts for others.

In a similar way, God exists for you alone. That is to say, He loves you as though you were the only person He created. You do not have to share God's love as if it were divided among many others. It is entirely focused on you individually and on others individually, and He can do this because His love is infinite. The psalmist proclaims[26],

> Lord, you have probed me, you know me: you know when I sit and stand; you understand my thoughts from afar. You sift through my travels and my rest; with all my ways you are familiar. Even before a word is on my tongue, Lord, you know it all.

Do not be jealous of others. There is no reason. He is delighted in your existence, and the gifts which He has endowed you with are unique to you. You manifest God's love for the world in a way that no one else can. He sees you in this unique way and loves you with all of His infinite goodness.

Neither should you think that God only loves you if you have great successes in your life. True success is found in clinging to God's love and trusting in it. It is His love, after all, which will transform our hearts. It is His love which gives us meaning and dignity as persons. Proverbs tells us[27], "Trust in the Lord with all

---

[25] Jeremiah 1:5
[26] Psalm 139:1-6
[27] Proverbs 3:5-6

your heart, on your own intelligence do not rely; In all your ways be mindful of him, and he will make straight your paths." His love remains the absolute center and focus of life. In the end, it is the only thing that really matters and the only thing that we can count on, and in finding this, we also find the value of prayer.

Yet, too often the world can rattle our contemplative life with doubts, confusions, guilt, and temptations. We can only find peace in these situations by returning to our relationship with God in the silence of our hearts, and allowing Him to remind us what we mean to Him. To say with Mary[28], "May it be done to me according to your word," gives our souls peace. To sit in the presence of the Lord and reflect on His love gives our souls joy. Life is no more complicated than bringing our concerns and troubles to Him and sitting at His feet. The psalmist states[29], "Say to the Lord, 'My refuge and fortress, my God in whom I trust.' He will rescue you from the fowler's snare, from the destroying plague, He will shelter you with his pinions, and under his wings you may take refuge; his faithfulness is a protecting shield." This is the road to happiness and fulfillment as a person. When we lean on Him with all of our being, we can find the deepest desire and fulfillment of our hearts, which is to be united with Him who is life, and to give our life to others.

✳✳✳

Find Your Meaning

The hills rolled around me as contemplation washed over me. I was in a field so large that I couldn't see the end of it in any direction. During this time, a butterfly landed on the grass in front of me. "Where do you find your meaning?" I asked the butterfly.

"In this field," she said, "it is my playground where I can flutter to and fro and be myself."

---

[28] Luke 1:38
[29] Psalm 91:2-4

Then came a crow, and I asked, "Where do you find your meaning?"

"In this field," she replied, "where I can get away to reflect on things for a while."

Next came a rabbit, and I asked again. "In this field," she said, "where I was raised, and where I now raise my little ones."

After they had left, I asked the field, "Where do you find your meaning?"

"It is found in the butterflies, the crows, and the rabbits," he replied.

Part Two:
Receive His Love

Prayer is the night sky as the moon casts its guiding glow, and the mystery of the stars draws us outside of ourselves and into the universe beyond.

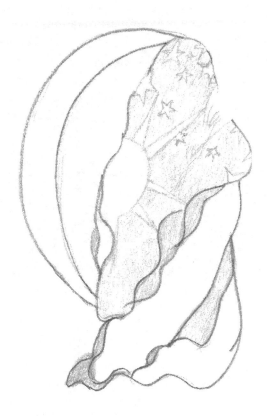

In part one of this book, we focused on understanding the truth of God's love for us and its positive effects on our lives. Now, we will focus on opening our palms to receive this great love and so to find the fullness of our selves. Only our recognition of God's love for us can motivate us to open ourselves in this way. A list of laws and regulations can never do this, nor can feelings of guilt. These things can never be the foundation of our spiritual life. Only His love can be the cause for which we humble ourselves and receive this gift from Him.

At times, we are very conscious of our sinfulness, our ugliness, and our bitterness, and we are weighed down by our guilt. When we think of God's love during these moments, He seems remote. We wonder how He could possibly love us, but He does, and He is already there with us in our repentance. As we continue to look upon His heart, pierced for us, we will grow in the areas of charity, purity, and humility. The wounds in our hearts will continue to heal. Reflect on John's account of the passion, where he says[30],

> So, the soldiers came and broke the legs of the first and then of the other one who was crucified with Jesus. But when they came to Jesus and saw that he was already dead, they did not break his legs, but one soldier thrust his lance into his side, and immediately blood and water flowed out.

It is Mark who notes that the centurion, upon seeing the Savior's wounded heart, exclaims[31], "Truly this man was the Son of God."

Not only does God see the goodness that is in us now, but He also sees the fulfillment of our goodness and our person. He longs to see us as He created us to be, to the point of giving Himself up on the cross, and our hearts long for this too. When we keep focused on Him therefore, instead of on our own weaknesses, His grace heals us.

God loves us just as much with our imperfections as without them. But, because He loves us so much, He desires our

---

[30] John 19:32-34
[31] Mark 15:39

complete fulfillment. His love draws us to purity of heart. We ought not obsess over our faults, but focus on Him whose love knows no bounds. Never be led to believe that God's love for you is diminished in any way. Remember Jesus' words in Luke's gospel[32], "I have not come to call the righteous to repentance but sinners." Trust in His love for you. Count on it. Act on it. Live it. That is the beginning of a life of faith and sanctity.

Yes, we will be happy when we become pure of heart. We will be happy when we have cast off the chains binding us to darkness and our eyes forever gaze upon the light. The psalmist cries out to God[33], "Cleanse me with hyssop, that I may be pure; wash me, and I will be whiter than snow. You will let me hear gladness and joy; the bones you have crushed will rejoice." He wishes to bestow these graces upon us, and in time, we shall receive them. He longs to see us raise to the stature of our fullest self, yet He is patient. We must learn from His patience and see that He loves us as we are. We must not be in a hurry to fix ourselves. We grow slowly, just as the moon slowly glides across the night sky, and it is in this growth that we learn virtue. Our prayer life helps us achieve this.

Remember that, for God, to be and to love are one in the same. When we contemplate His Being, we realize that He holds all that we are and all that we sense in Himself, and yet He remains shrouded in a silent Love. Recall His words to Job[34],

> Where were you when I founded the earth? Tell me, if you have understanding. Who determined its size? Surely you know? Who stretched out the measuring line for it? Into what were its pedestals sunk, and who laid its cornerstone, while the morning stars sang together and all the sons of God shouted for joy?

It is because His love is infinite and inexhaustible that this mystery is welcomed in our hearts and draws us ever deeper. We can also

---

[32] Luke 5:32
[33] Psalm 51:9-10
[34] Job 38:4-7

contemplate the particular aspects of His love. These aspects include truth, beauty, goodness, mercy, peace, joy, life, light, justice, and countless more. We can rest in these. His mercy, for example, can heal and teach true repentance and true forgiveness, if only we would take the time to rest there. Remember how God has been merciful to you, and then you can give that same mercy to others. Rest in His truth, and you will find the security of an impenetrable shield. Rest in His beauty and be filled with wonder at His creation. It is good for us to rest in Him in contemplation. When we seek Him with all our hearts, we will find everything we long for. We are plunging ever deeper into this mystery.

God is so close to us that we don't need to use words to speak with Him. If we wish, we can simply offer Him our very selves in the silence of this moment as a whisper from our hearts. He calls us to rest with Him – to unite our yolk with His. In Matthew's gospel, Jesus implores us[35], "Come to me, all you who labor and are burdened, and I will give you rest. Take my yoke upon you and learn from me, for I am meek and humble of heart; and you will find rest for yourselves. For my yoke is easy, and my burden light." This has a great advantage when we find it difficult to put our state of being into words or when we find the use of words to be bothersome at a particular moment. He is so close to us that we can be assured He already knows about it, and we can offer it to Him in trusting silence.

In our prayer life, we do not seek to understand someone as much as to be with someone. It is through being with God - spending time with Him in silence and conversing with Him in our hearts - that we come to know Him. He is bringing us into the warmth of a mystery ever deeper and wider. It is something that we live more than we understand, but we still catch glimpses of its truth and beauty. In this life, we already share in the mystery of the Resurrection through our hope, and one day, we will see Him face to face and know eternal joy.

---

[35] Matthew 11:28-30

***

Sounds

One very early morning, after Lauds, a monk asked me to follow him outside. The moon was shining full, and he asked me if I would jump to it with him. So, we did.

He invited me to spend six months on the dark side of the moon, listening to the sounds from the beginning of Creation. He then told me that I should afterward walk to the other side of the moon and listen to the sounds from the earth. He said he would be back in a year, and he left me there, on the moon, alone.

I did what he said. For the first six months I listened to the sounds from the beginning of Creation. I heard the silence of 'Good' and the beautiful harmony of 'Very Good'. Then I walked to the other side and listened to sounds from the earth. I heard much discord and chaos, but under this, I still discerned the silence of 'Good' and the harmony of 'Very Good'.

At the end of the year, the monk came back and asked me what I heard. I told him, and he said that my listening was well done. Then he asked, "Did you hear how it ends?"

Prayer is water trickling as mildly as a stream, yet flowing as strong as a river. It is as light as a drop, yet as powerful as a waterfall. It is as still as a lake in the early morning even when it is as stormy as an ocean.

In the last chapter, we began looking at things that can cause us to block God out of our lives, such as feelings of guilt. We will continue in this chapter to work on opening ourselves up to receive the love that God has for us. There are many things that can prevent us from being fully open to God's love. It is true that sinfulness keeps us from Him, but dwelling upon our sinfulness is a far greater inhibitor. When we focus on our sinfulness, we are turned away from God, and focused on ourselves, although it can feel like humility. True humility, however, focuses not on our own sinfulness, but on Divine Mercy. The great story to tell is not of our failures, rather, it is the story of God's goodness and forgiveness that should seize our hearts and minds.

In all things and all times remember that to approach God is to approach pure and perfect Love. Jesus did not die on the cross so that we would feel guilty or ashamed, but so that we might come to know His forgiveness and unconditional love. That is why He calls us to repentance. Consider Jesus' story of the prodigal son in Luke's Gospel. The father doesn't even let the son finish his intended apology[36] before he says with impatient earnestness[37], "Quickly bring the finest robe and put it on him; put a ring on his finger and sandals on his feet. Take the fattened calf and slaughter it. Then let us celebrate with a feast, because this son of mine was dead, and has come to life again; he was lost, and has been found." When you go to God to seek His forgiveness, therefore, go with contrite confidence in His infinite mercy. When you speak to Him in your heart, do it with the greatest of trust and honesty. Know that He loves you deeply and nothing you can do will ever change that. He will never disappoint you.

God's love for us is far too often underestimated and underappreciated. He is eager to forgive and to bring us back into His family when we fall. Jesus says in John's Gospel[38], "God did not send his Son into the world to condemn the world, but that the

---

[36] To see this, compare Luke 15:18-19 with Luke 15:21
[37] Luke 15:22-24
[38] John 3:17

world might be saved through him." He is eager to give us our heart's desire. Consider the Nativity and how He came to us as a vulnerable little child. He did not come down in fiery condemnation, but in innocent sleep. Consider His crucifixion, and how He died in order to restore our salvation. Consider how He comes to us in the Eucharist, silent under the appearance of bread and wine. This is certainly not a God who came to condemn us, but to seek the lost, to love the lonely, and to heal the addicted. He created us, knowing that we would put Him to death, because He would rather face death than be without us. His love for us never ceases and never changes. What was from all eternity will be for all eternity. God is love, and He has come to give us life.

God is even able to overcome our mistakes and make a new creation out of our repentant hearts. He knew from all eternity that we would do sinful things, and in His perfection, He knew how to bring about life and hope within us. Evidence of this is found in His crucifixion and resurrection, bringing life out of death. God speaks through the prophet Isaiah saying[39], "See, I am creating new heavens and a new earth; The former things shall not be remembered nor come to mind. Instead, shout for joy and be glad forever in what I am creating." Just as water purifies and cleanses us, so God can cleanse and purify our hearts such that they are even more beautiful than before.

Even in our individual lives, when we are repentant and open to His grace, He is able to bring about goodness in the midst of our mistakes. Indeed, we sometimes have to make mistakes in order for us to learn from them and grow in holiness. God has accounted for all the bad things which we have done, and we will see Him miraculously use them for our own advancement in holiness, and for other's advancement as well, if we only allow His grace to penetrate our repentant hearts.

Therefore, we should not focus on our state of sinfulness, but on God's infinite love, meeting us just where we are. The former will inevitably lead us inward towards self-hatred and

---

[39] Isaiah 65:17-18

arrogance toward others. The latter will lead us outward toward love of others and of God. Jesus says in Luke's Gospel[40], "I tell you, in just the same way there will be more joy in heaven over one sinner who repents than over ninety-nine righteous people who have no need of repentance." Focusing on God's love for us, despite our sins and human condition, is the source of our spiritual growth.

This infinitely merciful God is in control of our lives, and this should relieve us of all our worries. He is all-powerful, all-knowing, and all-loving. What have we to fear who follow in His footsteps? When we give God our full confidence we can say, "Foolish worries!" Then we will have the proper perspective on things. Recall the Lord's words to Joshua[41], "Do not fear nor be dismayed, for the Lord, your God, is with you wherever you go." Suffering and difficulty inevitably occur in our lives, but His grace is enough for us to remain close to Him on the road to our eternal home.

We can allow His love to penetrate the darkest parts of our soul where we are afraid, worried, or doubting, and be at peace. Remember that the road to Calvary is also the road to victory. Again, the prophet Isaiah speaks the comforting word of God[42], "I chose you, I have not rejected you—Do not fear: I am with you; do not be anxious: I am your God. I will strengthen you, I will help you, I will uphold you with my victorious right hand." On this journey, we can also find shelter and security in the Heart of Mary, our spiritual mother, who knows the depth of suffering that we face. We can allow her to purify us in the loving furnace of her Immaculate Heart. Therefore, we can be at peace. Our soul is loved and precious in her eyes and the eyes of her Son.

✳✳✳

---

[40] Luke 15:7
[41] Joshua 1:9
[42] Isaiah 41:9-10

The River

I was sitting with a monk by a large river which flowed steadily along as did the pace of our conversation. At one point, I started to tell him all the reasons why God couldn't love me. He stopped me and said, "Your faults and failings are like these rocks. God's love is like this river. The river flows around them, over them, and eventually washes them away."

But I was far too arrogant to give up so easily, so I said with sarcasm, "Ah, I see," and in my frustration, I started throwing rocks into the river for each of my faults, naming them as I threw. The monk sat there smiling and watched as the rocks piled up high enough to completely block the flow of the river.

"Now," he said, "Who was concerned about those rocks? You or the river?"

Prayer is a cup, formed by its maker to give that which it receives.

In the previous chapter, we examined how we can block God's love by focusing on our sinfulness instead of His mercy. In this chapter, we will continue looking at how to receive God's love and remove those obstacles which block His light from reaching the depths of our being. Even though our hearts are not fully pure, we should not be afraid to offer them to Christ, for this is the only way that we can be healed. In John's first letter he states[43], "If we acknowledge our sins, he is faithful and just and will forgive our sins and cleanse us from every wrongdoing." God understands that an imperfect heart is all we have to offer Him, and He gladly accepts us as we are.

No matter what state we find our hearts in, we must offer them to the loving hands of Christ, which are always reaching out for us. Consider the prophet Ezekiel speaking the Word of the Lord[44], "I will give you a new heart, and a new spirit I will put within you. I will remove the heart of stone from your flesh and give you a heart of flesh." Indeed, His love comes at us like waves, again and again, always seeking to soften our hearts. We must not let our guilt or our pride get the better of us. If we have gone hours, days, months, years, or even decades without thinking about Him, we must not be discouraged. We need His love. Without it, we are left to the storms of insanity and despair to dispense with us. As often as we think about it, we ought to hand over the state of our hearts to the merciful love of God. These prayerful moments keep us close to the source of hope because they open the door of our hearts to Him and invite Him to stay with us.

We must accept the fact that our lives are often riddled with imperfections. We cannot overcome them with the shear effort of our will. Only the slow transfusion of His grace into our souls, as we continue to gaze upon Him with open hearts, can turn our imperfections into sources of life. This is a lesson in humility and a lesson in God's mercy and goodness. His love for us is

---

[43] 1 John 1:9
[44] Ezekiel 36:26

unaffected by our imperfections, faults, and failures. He is patient with us, and in His mercy, He calls out to us over and over after we have left His way, just as He leaves the ninety-nine sheep to search for the one[45]. By now, though, we may be wondering what we have to do in order to receive God's love. What do we have to do to earn it?

Then again, we may have realized the answer. God's love is already penetrating our being at every moment. We just need to say, "yes," in the silence of our hearts. These moments of "yes", in turn, become our prayer. Then, and only then, can we learn to love others with the same love with which Christ has loved us. Consider what St. Paul says in his first letter to the Corinthians[46],

> If I speak in human and angelic tongues but do not have love, I am a resounding gong or a clashing cymbal. And if I have the gift of prophecy and comprehend all mysteries and all knowledge; if I have all faith so as to move mountains but do not have love, I am nothing. If I give away everything I own, and if I hand my body over so that I may boast but do not have love, I gain nothing.

One of the last things which Jesus said to His disciples before His passion was[47], "This I command you: love one another." He wants us to give the love that we have received from Him. We can open our hearts to others and pour out His love to them because they too are like us. They too are vulnerable and need to experience the love of Christ from us.

However, it is not good to compare ourselves with others, even if they are saints. They lived in their own time, with their own experiences, and their own challenges. Each of us is an unrepeatable person with a different purpose. Each of us has our own spirituality, our own life, and our own mission, just as each cup has a unique shape with which to give its contents to another. We are all called to be unique saints. Therefore, if we try to

---

[45] Luke 15:4-6
[46] 1 Corinthians 13:1-3
[47] John 15: 17

imitate others and measure up to them, we will always fail. We are not called to be them, but to be us. Keep in mind that God loves you simply in that you exist. You don't have to do great things in order to please Him. With God, there is no pressure to "be somebody". We just have to be, and He loves us in that. As He speaks to us through the Song of Songs[48], "Let me see your face, let me hear your voice, for your voice is sweet, and your face is lovely."

Even though are lives in this world will come to an end, God, His love, and our being will always remain. This is what really matters. Here we find a place of peaceful stillness that is always accessible, always tranquil, even if our thoughts and the world around us are agitated. It is the meeting place where God is holding our souls, so sweetly and gently, in their existence - it is the place of prayer. As Jesus cries out in the Temple of Jerusalem during the Feast of Tabernacles[49], "Let anyone who thirsts come to me and drink." This is the deep and hidden reality within each of us, at the very core of our being, and it is here that we find fulfillment and peace.

✳✳✳

For You

When I was on retreat at a monastery, I asked the monk who was directing it, "what do I have to do in order to receive God's love?"

---

[48] Song of Songs 2:14
[49] John 7:37

All he said to me then was, "You are the cup."

That night he came into my room and woke me up by shattering a porcelain cup on the floor of my cell. Then he poured water out of a pitcher and onto the remains of the shattered cup, saying to me, "My love for you." Then he cleaned up the mess and left. He did the same thing the next night, and the next night, and the next night, until the last night of my retreat.

On the last night he came into my room and woke me up. Then he poured water into a cup that was glued together from the pieces of the broken ones, and gave it to me saying, "My love for you." Then he reminded me saying, "You are the cup," and left the room. The cup leaks a little bit, but I won't ever get rid of it.

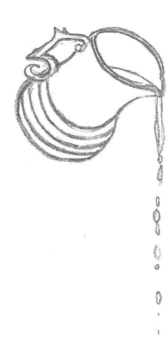

Prayer is a stone in the desert standing durable and steady amidst the purifying terrain.

Over the last three chapters, we have discussed how to remain open to God's love despite our sinfulness, what we have to do (or rather don't have to do) to earn His love, and the importance of giving that love to others. In this chapter, we will examine how to remain open to His love in times of spiritual dryness and unforgiveness. Let us begin our discussion on spiritual dryness by noting that we shouldn't worry about distractions in our prayer time. God is not bothered by them. He is happy in the simple fact that we are making the effort to be with Him. It is the effort that is important, not the results. If He wanted, He could make us attentive and focused all the time, but for reasons ultimately unknown to us, He allows us to be distracted. Even in our distractions, we can share our distracted thoughts with Him and listen to His voice in our hearts. He may have advice for us about the subject of our distractions, and that may be the reason for them. It may be that He is trying to get us to think about a problem in a new way. In any case, it is best to let them be absorbed into the silence of our prayer. It is only when we become worried about our distractions that we become lost in them.

What do we do, then, when our relationship with God becomes stale and boring? The immediate way to address the situation is to give it to Him. We can offer Him our moments of boredom and our distaste for dryness. That it is all we really have to offer Him at that moment, and so it pleases Him. He will not remove our dryness immediately, but He helps us to continue on our way. We shouldn't be afraid to be humble, open, and honest with Him. We can share our most embarrassing and foolish struggles with Him and trust Him to understand. As Peter says in his first letter[50], "for a little while you may have to suffer through various trials, so that the genuineness of your faith, more precious than gold that is perishable even though tested by fire, may prove to be for praise, glory, and honor at the revelation of Jesus Christ." God certainly has a plan for us that we do not understand, and all

---

[50] 1 Peter 1:6-7

of this plays its part, just as a stone does not understand how it will be beautifully shaped by its terrain.

It is important for us to remember that to be alive is to be loved by God. His love is like the sun in that the sun is always shining. It may be obscured by clouds, it may be merely reflected off the moon, or it may be entirely lost in the darkness of night, but it is still shining. In the same way, we may not feel the presence of God's love in our souls, but it is there. It is present in all of creation, it is the source of our existence, and it is the root of our desire to grow closer to Him. These things are evidence that God still loves us beyond what we can or cannot sense. The prophet Jeremiah states[51], "The Lord's acts of mercy are not exhausted, his compassion is not spent; They are renewed each morning—great is your faithfulness! The Lord is my portion, I tell myself, therefore I will hope in him." We can make an effort to be at peace then, and to trust in Him, for the sun is always shining.

We must also strive to remember that God has placed His Divine Life within us. From all eternity, He has known each of us individually and has prepared a home for us in Heaven. He cares for us more than we could know. God is not distant, but near to us on our journey. He sustains us as we are led back home. Saint Paul says to the Greeks in the Acts of the Apostles[52],

> He made from one the whole human race to dwell on the entire surface of the earth, and he fixed the ordered seasons and the boundaries of their regions, so that people might seek God, even perhaps grope for him and find him, though indeed he is not far from any one of us. For 'In him we live and move and have our being,' as even some of your poets have said.

God did not put us in this world to punish us for our sinfulness, but so that we might learn to walk with Him in faith. He is longing for our wandering to come to an end, just as we are. What awaits us is

---

[51] Lamentations 3:22-24
[52] Acts 17:26-28

nothing less than the fullness of Divine Life, the restoration of creation, and our eternal homeland.

All of us fall on this journey back to Him. We must be mindful of our brothers and sisters who are wounded, and who, because of their wounds, hurt us. We must remember that their hurtful acts stem from their wounded nature, and we should be generous in our forgiveness, just as Jesus tells Peter to forgive[53], "not seven times but seventy-seven times." We can learn to show great patience towards others in their imperfections and weaknesses, just as the Lord has been so patient with us and our wounded hearts. We can give them the room necessary to allow the Holy Spirit to work in their lives by forgiving them. Recall Jesus' words to the Pharisees in John's Gospel as they were preparing to stone the woman caught in adultery[54], "Let the one among you who is without sin be the first to throw a stone at her." We know that the Lord loves our enemies infinitely, just as He loves us, and we should try to look upon them with this same love.

Unforgiveness, on the other hand, keeps us from fully growing in our spiritual life because it keeps us from receiving God's love to the fullest extent. It hardens our hearts and acts as a barrier to God's love. When others wound us, it is important to acknowledge that they are struggling to live out charity in their own lives just as we are. We ought to give them the spiritual space that they need to continue on the path of love, or perhaps to even find the path of love, and that space can only come through our forgiveness. Consider Jonah's words when he was disappointed at seeing God's mercy directed toward the enemies of Israel[55], "This is why I fled at first toward Tarshish. I knew that you are a gracious and merciful God, slow to anger, abounding in kindness, repenting of punishment." This is how we can show love to those who hurt us: by learning from Divine Mercy. We can forgive them,

---

[53] Matthew 18:22
[54] John 8:7
[55] Jonah 4:2

gently providing the space and time necessary for their spiritual advancement while we continue on that path ourselves.

∗∗∗

Mercy Stones

On one of my retreats in the desert, I was walking around, and I came across a huge rock in the middle of all that sand. On the top, it was written: "The Stone of Judgment". As I looked closer I saw the names of all the people I knew, and underneath their names were lists of their sins and faults. As I took the information in, the wind of the desert began to whisper curses and condemnations directed toward them.

When I reached out to touch it, I noticed how easily chips crumbled away from the giant stone. I filled my bag with them so that I could hand them out and help others by pointing out their sinfulness. When my bag was filled, I left thinking about how successful this retreat was.

After a while, though, the whispering desert began to tell me all my faults! It told me all my sins and judged me and condemned me and laughed at me for days. Weeks went by and then months. I couldn't stand that wind. I felt so embarrassed, so ashamed, so angry, tortured with guilt and sorrow.

After too much of this, I began to look for a Stone of Mercy. I figured there must be one in the desert somewhere, and sure enough, I eventually found it. It was also a big stone like the Stone of Judgment. But when I looked, it just had one word written on it: "Mercy". When I got close, the whispers stopped. All was calm and peaceful in my mind. I wanted to rest there forever, but I knew I couldn't.

I noticed that this stone also chipped away quite easily, so I emptied my bag of judgment stones, and they turned to blood in the sand. Then I filled my bag with mercy stones. As I walked away, the desert wind whispered words of forgiveness, calm, and love into my ears. Now that I'm back in the world, if anybody annoys or wounds me, I just give them a stone of mercy. If I ever get close to running out of those stones, I know right where to go.

**Part Three:
Trust in Him**

Prayer is a battle that we must lose. It is a fight for no other reason than to give in to Him who is Love.

Part one of our journey examined the ways in which God's love is accessible to us, and part two examined the obstacles that can get in the way of receiving His love. Now, in part three, we will examine how to trust in God, even in times of suffering and spiritual darkness. Particularly, in this chapter, we will focus on not giving into discouragement and despair when we see how little we have progressed in our spiritual lives. We ought to trust in Divine Mercy to meet us where we are and draw us ever closer.

We shouldn't despair that we have not yet achieved total union with God. We need not despair when we continually find ourselves in a state of sinfulness. We are a work in progress, and it is a long and arduous work. We fall again and again in the same areas, but Jesus is always there to pick us back up. We are making progress. We are still striving for that complete union with God's will. That is the most important part of our journey, that we desire and continue to walk with the Lord, keeping our eyes focused on His mercy and His love. Recall how God leads the people of Israel to the promised land. The book of Exodus states[56], "The Lord preceded them, in the daytime by means of a column of cloud to show them the way, and at night by means of a column of fire to give them light." Likewise, our prayer reminds us of His presence and His loving guidance. In the Gospel of Luke, Jesus teaches us how to pray[57], and the first word of this prayer is "Father". This is to remind us that God is our Father who loves us and takes care of us on our journey. He looks at our effort more than our outcome. We must not become frustrated with ourselves, rather we should patiently follow Him, day and night, until we have arrived at our eternal home.

We cannot overcome our sinfulness through shear willpower. Our virtue can only grow with love, and that can only come from God. It is His grace alone that can change us, and we find His grace in prayer. This process takes place by allowing Him to touch the weakness of our hearts. It is good to be patient and

---

[56] Exodus 13:21
[57] Luke 11:2

humble in this, trusting in Him to bring about change when He is ready, continuing to offer ourselves to Him, surrendering our battles to Him.

That is the role of the will - to bring all that we are as a person, both weaknesses and gifts, to Him in trust. This is the way to freedom – that we acknowledge our wounded nature as well as God's healing power and His unconditional love. He loves the pure and the impure equally. The difference is that one has been transformed into this love while the other is still being purified. Be as open as possible, even if it's just a tiny bit, to that transforming grace, which is His loving gaze, looking upon you with mercy. Still, when we fall into sin, we can run quickly to Our Father, knowing that He wants to heal us. Trust in His boundless mercy. There is no reason to be afraid, He is with us through everything. He is more deeply aware of our own weaknesses than we are, and He is far more compassionate and patient than we can imagine.

Every trial, every setback, every temptation, every suffering is another chance for us to deepen our faith in the Lord, and to give ourselves further to Him. He allows us to feel helpless in overcoming our weaknesses so that He might draw us to Himself and give us His Divine Life. These moments are in our lives for this purpose, so that we can unite ourselves to Him in a deeper and more loving way.

Consider the lover in the Song of Songs[58], who says,
I rose to open for my lover, my hands dripping myrrh: My fingers, flowing myrrh upon the handles of the lock. I opened for my lover—but my lover had turned and gone! At his leaving, my soul sank. I sought him, but I did not find him; I called out after him, but he did not answer me.
Yet the lover pursues the object of her desire in hope, despite her confusion about his absence. Following this example, we can give our heart to the Lord as it is, trusting that He is at work, even though we don't feel it or understand it. That is all He is asking of

---

[58] Song of Songs 5:5-6

us during these difficult moments of prayer when He seems to have vanished from our lives – to offer Him our wounded hearts in trust.

It is important for us to learn to open our hearts to Christ in times of doubt. When we feel for a moment that we cannot continue trusting Christ, when we are tempted to turn away from Him, when we have a distaste for our life with Him, when we feel He has abandoned us, we can still allow Him access to our hearts. He is not angry. He understands our struggles and doubts. Remember that Jesus[59], "remained in the desert for forty days, tempted by Satan." It is our faith in His love and our gratitude for the gift of our lives that will allow our relationship with Him to heal. After all, God wants to give us the peace that we desire. It won't be long before our hearts regain their peace. In the meantime, ponder the good things He has done for you and the beauty of the place He is leading you to.

Even when these storms of trial and doubt surge upon us suddenly and with great force, we can hold tight to Jesus in faith, trusting that He is there in the depths of our hearts as the waves crash upon us. And when we ask for His help, we ought to ask with the greatest faith in His love for us. Consider the wavering faith of the apostles in Matthew's Gospel when they were with Jesus in their boat[60],

> Suddenly a violent storm came up on the sea, so that the boat was being swamped by waves; but he was asleep. They came and woke him, saying, 'Lord, save us! We are perishing!' He said to them, 'Why are you terrified, O you of little faith?' Then he got up, rebuked the winds and the sea, and there was great calm.

Have hope, for the dawn will come. Even still, when you fall, don't despair! He is with you, ready to start again, ready to accept you, and He loves you just the same.

---

[59] Mark 1:13
[60] Matthew 8:24-26

To this end, it is helpful for our days to be filled with moments of prayer by turning our hearts to Christ and offering ourselves to Him. These little moments point us in the right direction and are stepping stones to the full union of our will with His. In the first letter of John[61], we read, "There is no fear in love, but perfect love drives out fear." Take all your fears and struggles to Jesus and allow Him to be with you. Allow them to soak in His love for you until they dissolve in His peace.

✳✳✳

Divine Breath

During one of my retreats, I noticed that my temptations and doubts were turning into black flies in my cell. Every time I

---

[61] 1 John 4:18

had a new temptation or doubt, another fly would go buzzing around the room! Pretty soon, I was battling a whole swarm of invaders, so I asked an old monk what to do. He walked into my cell and opened the window. Then he took a deep breath and blew all the flies out of the room with one big exhale. Lastly, he said to me, "Always and at all times leave the window of your heart open to the Divine Breath." I never closed my cell window during that retreat either.

Prayer is a wound that will never heal. It keeps us in humble need of His healing hands.

In this chapter, we will continue to look at the things in our lives, such as bitterness and doubt, which can keep us from trusting in God. We ought to be aware of these things because they damage our relationship with Him and make it hard to have faith in Him. During these moments, we don't believe He could possibly love us, and so we become angry. Our hearts become hardened and we don't want to pray. Yet that is what we must do. At these times, we must lay our hearts softly in His hands, and recognize how gently He holds them.

This life can be very gritty, very raw, and sometimes far too real for us to handle our emotions. There can be so much suffering, tragedy, addiction, fear, anxiety, confusion, and loneliness in our lives. But we must not be afraid of facing these things. That is why spending silent time in prayer with God is so important. Consider the Gospel of Luke when Jesus' parents find Him after He went missing[62],

> When his parents saw him, they were astonished, and his
> mother said to him, 'Son, why have you done this to us?
> Your father and I have been looking for you with great
> anxiety.' And he said to them, 'Why were you looking for
> me? Did you not know that I must be in my Father's house?'
> But they did not understand what he said to them. He went
> down with them and came to Nazareth, and was obedient
> to them; and his mother kept all these things in her heart.

We need to find a silent space in our hearts where we can ponder just as Mary did, and in that space, we need to allow Christ to enter into our wounds.

Only God can be our true companion and guide to these depths because only He understands us completely, and only He can fully heal us. In these depths, we can allow Him to touch our wounds with His wounds in the same way that lovers are able to open their heart's depths to each other. This is the spiritual communion that we long for, and it is born in the stillness of silence. Do not be afraid and do not be ashamed, or rather give

---

[62] Luke 2:48-51

Him your shame and your fear, and allow His love to transform them.

The voice of God can be easily drowned out by the noise of this world, since He is so gentle with us and greatly respects our freedom. He comes only in the silence of our hearts. Recall the book of Kings, when God visits Elijah[63],

> Then the Lord said: Go out and stand on the mountain before the Lord; the Lord will pass by. There was a strong and violent wind rending the mountains and crushing rocks before the Lord—but the Lord was not in the wind; after the wind, an earthquake—but the Lord was not in the earthquake; after the earthquake, fire—but the Lord was not in the fire; after the fire, a light silent sound. When he heard this, Elijah hid his face in his cloak and went out and stood at the entrance of the cave. A voice said to him, Why are you here, Elijah?

We must strive to create a silent space in our hearts, where we can listen to His whispers and be with Him.

It is in this silence that God teaches us about His love. He teaches us how to deal with our emotions and fears. He quenches our loneliness. He channels our frustrations and failures into a positive outcome. The value of our silence is that He speaks to our hearts, calming them, soothing them, encouraging them, and healing our wounds. Silence is the breath of prayer where He fills us with life and grace.

When things begin to bother us, and we become frustrated, or hurt, or afraid, we can take them to Jesus in our hearts. He is a constant refuge from the winds of the world that blow against us. As the psalmist states[64], "God is our refuge and our strength, an ever-present help in distress. Thus, we do not fear, though earth be shaken and mountains quake to the depths of the sea." In the depths of our hearts, where His love keeps us in existence, He is

---

[63] 1 Kings 19:11-13
[64] Psalm 46:2-3

there, waiting to receive us with open arms. We find His love. We find His peace. Our trials bring us to the source of life.

When we turn to the Lord in times of need we are, in effect, longing for His presence in our hearts – His love, His mercy, His peace. Without His presence, we could never possess these qualities in our hearts, indeed, we could not exist. Spend time with Him, therefore, in times of distress, when your love is weak, for He is the source of peace. Whether or not we feel His presence makes little difference when we have faith in His unchanging love.

We find the source of our strength in our brokenness. Saint Paul says in his second letter to the Corinthians[65], "I am content with weaknesses, insults, hardships, persecutions, and constraints, for the sake of Christ; for when I am weak, then I am strong." When we are suffering or distressed we find our true comfort in God. It is in moments of trial and anguish that we grow by putting our faith in Him who loves us. That is the value of our suffering. It prompts us to seek and to find Him in our hearts. Then He becomes our companion for the journey. It is a wonderful thing when we discover God amidst the darkness of our lives. From that moment on, we are never alone.

There is nothing we can do to deserve our existence or our Savior, nor do we have anything to offer Him who laid down His life for us. We are ultimately empty handed and needy. But all He asks is that we place ourselves in His palms to receive His gifts of love and mercy. We cannot earn these things. He simply loves us as we are. God says through His prophet Isaiah[66], "Can a mother forget her infant, be without tenderness for the child of her womb? Even should she forget, I will never forget you. See, upon the palms of my hands I have engraved you." He has engraved us in the wounds of His hands, pierced to give us life. Life, in the end, is simply a matter of being, and He is not asking us to be anything other than what we already are: poor, wounded, and loved.

---

[65] 2 Corinthians 12:10
[66] Isaiah 49:15-16

Our hearts are vulnerable because they require love to grow just as our lungs require oxygen to breathe. In order to be loved, we must open our hearts, and it is then that they become susceptible to humiliations and wounds. But we must not be afraid to be vulnerable to Jesus. It is necessary for us to expose the darkest, most unbelieving, and most bitter parts of ourselves to His love so that He can set us free from them. Consider the Gospel of Mark's account of Jesus' exorcism of a boy possessed by demons. Jesus tells the boy's father[67],

> "Everything is possible to one who has faith." Then the boy's father cried out, "I do believe, help my unbelief!" Jesus, on seeing a crowd rapidly gathering, rebuked the unclean spirit and said to it, "Mute and deaf spirit, I command you: come out of him and never enter him again!" Shouting and throwing the boy into convulsions, it came out. He became like a corpse, which caused many to say, "He is dead!" But Jesus took him by the hand, raised him, and he stood up.

Too often we have wounds and doubts that we try to hide from God and even from ourselves. The light of Christ can be intimidating, but it is like soothing balm to our vulnerable hearts.

✳✳✳

Pierced Like His

I once visited a monastery where I noticed a monk with the word "FOOL" stamped in dark black ink across his forehead. One day, I got up the courage to ask him about it. He told me that his

---

[67] Mark 9:23-27

brother monks had done this to him because he could never do anything right. "I was terribly humiliated," he said, "I felt so worthless, and I spent many nights feeling helplessly alone. But this brought me right to the Heart of Christ. Who else could I go to for encouragement and friendship? The only way His love could find its way into my heart was when it was pierced like His."

Prayer is a tomb, empty and void, where we are laid in the death of our sinfulness.

The last two chapters led us to explore the ways in which we can continue trusting in God through times of doubt and find Him in the midst of our difficulties. In this chapter, we will examine the spiritual side of suffering in more depth. Suffering is, and will always be, a mystery to us in this life. It is not something that we can rationalize or come to understand from an objective point of view. Rather, it calls for great faith and hope to stay rooted in the truth of God's goodness. We need to keep our gaze ever upon our relationship with Him and His love for us.

Keeping our relationship with God aflame through prayer is the only thing that can give us encouragement in times of suffering. We need to know that He loves us, and we need to hold onto that truth with all of our faith. Even in the darkest of hours it is a light that can burn brightly. That is why Saint Paul says in his letter to the Romans[68], "I am convinced that neither death, nor life, nor angels, nor principalities, nor present things, nor future things, nor powers, nor height, nor depth, nor any other creature will be able to separate us from the love of God in Christ Jesus our Lord." It is likely, though, that we will have bitterness or resistance in our hearts during these difficult moments, so we must try to open these areas of our hearts to Him and unite our suffering with His. We can use our prayerfulness to cast ourselves into His heart, pierced for us.

When all else is dark in despair, try to listen for the voice of peace and hope in your heart. God is there, whispering to you. We may pass long and dark hours when our faith seems to possess nothing. It is in this state that the psalmist cried[69], "How long, Lord? Will you utterly forget me? How long will you hide your face from me? How long must I carry sorrow in my soul, grief in my heart day after day? How long will my enemy triumph over me?" Recall also, the story of Abraham and how he climbed to the top of a mountain in Moriah to sacrifice his son. The author states[70],

---

[68] Romans 8:38-39
[69] Psalm 13:2-3
[70] Genesis 22:10-11

"Then Abraham reached out and took the knife to slaughter his son. But the angel of the Lord called to him from heaven, 'Abraham, Abraham!' 'Here I am,' he answered."

Abraham's, "Here I am," as a response to the angel of the Lord is more than just an answer. It is a cry rattling out from the very depths of his soul. It is the shout crumbling him to his knees and dropping his knife. At last, he understands, kneeling and weeping at his brokenness. God has pierced through the hardness that was covering his wounds, and now Divine healing can take place. God then speaks to Abraham through His angel[71], "I will bless you and make your descendants as countless as the stars of the sky and the sands of the seashore; your descendants will take possession of the gates of their enemies, and in your descendants, all the nations of the earth will find blessing, because you obeyed my command." Each breath he takes now will be the breath of a new life – a breath of prayer, a life united to God.

Even when our soul feels like it is in a dark spiritual tomb, His infinite love is still within us, guiding us. We are never separated from Him. We must know this beyond what our reason can understand. That is faith. We have experienced His love and know it to be true despite whatever our current circumstances may be. He is always seeking our happiness and emptying Himself out for our sake. Again, we cannot rationalize our suffering or fully understand how it works out for our good. Yet, we love Him precisely because He loved us first, and we recall His love in times of stillness.

Remember also that He is there in times of trial. Trust Him to be with you and strengthen you, even though you may not feel it. As the prophet Habakkuk states[72], "Though the fig tree does not blossom, and no fruit appears on the vine, though the yield of the olive fails and the terraces produce no nourishment, though the flocks disappear from the fold and there is no herd in the stalls, yet I will rejoice in the Lord and exult in my saving God." Allow the

---

[71] Genesis 22:17-18
[72] Habakkuk 3:17-18

words, "God is love", to be inscribed in your heart so that you take them with you wherever you go, even in the midst great distress.

When we are tired, we are tired with Christ. When we are sorrowful, we are sorrowful with Christ. When we are hurt, we are hurt with Christ. His wounds become our wounds, and our wounds become His wounds. His joys become our joys, and our joys become His joys. His will becomes our will, and our will becomes His will. The prophet Isaiah says[73], "It was our pain that he bore, our sufferings he endured." He desires this union with all His heart that He may bring us to life. It is through prayer, sacraments, and giving the gifts of ourselves to others that this union deepens. He calls us ever deeper into His loving embrace.

It is here that we come to understand that death is God's final embrace from which He shall never let go. It is only the beginning of a life united to Him. Luke's account of the burial of Jesus states that Joseph of Arimathea[74], "had taken the body down, he wrapped it in a linen cloth and laid him in a rock-hewn tomb in which no one had yet been buried. It was the day of preparation, and the sabbath was about to begin." As this life fades away, the veil of Heaven is torn, and He lifts us out of our limited world into the infinite one beyond. Then will come the day when we will forever gaze upon the face of God and see the New Creation in all its glory. We shall know the love of Christ warming our hearts for all eternity. Do not be afraid of suffering and death, for they can only bring you closer to Christ.

Now do you see the beauty in a crucifix? On the surface it seems absurd and fruitless – death by a cruel instrument of torture. Yet it is not beautiful because of what it is, rather its beauty lies in why it is. It is God become man, come to offer Himself to the point of a spear spilling out the last of His blood. It is our Savior sowing in us the seeds of life. It is the climax of His love. It is the opposite of fruitlessness and absurdity. It is His gift of Divine Life to humanity, and therein lies its beauty and the

---

[73] Isaiah 53:4
[74] Luke 23:53-54

healing which it can bring. Matthew's account of the passion states[75],

> From noon onward, darkness came over the whole land until three in the afternoon. And about three o'clock Jesus cried out in a loud voice, 'Eli, Eli, lema sabachthani?' which means, 'My God, my God, why have you forsaken me?' Some of the bystanders who heard it said, 'This one is calling for Elijah.' Immediately one of them ran to get a sponge; he soaked it in wine, and putting it on a reed, gave it to him to drink. But the rest said, 'Wait, let us see if Elijah comes to save him.' But Jesus cried out again in a loud voice, and gave up his spirit.

This is a paradox made clear by the resurrection: we are drawn to Him in His death because He is the source of life.

✻✻✻

The Dirt Path

A monk I once knew gave me the opportunity to spend one night in the Holy Sepulcher all by myself! I was meditating on the Passion of Christ, when suddenly everything around me turned dark, and there appeared two glowing doors. On one was written, "The Way of the Cross," and on the other, was written, "Short-cut to Heaven."

The first door I opened was "The Way of the Cross". As I peered inside, I saw a dirt path winding over the crest of a hill under a pitch-black sky. The air felt chilled and a howling wind

---

[75] Matthew 27:45-50

swirled around a desolate landscape. I shuddered and closed that door.

Next, I opened the "Short-cut to Heaven". It opened to a short white hallway and at the end of the hallway was a shining white door labeled "Heaven" in gold letters.

As I approached, drawn to that door, a lady in white appeared, and I stopped. She began to speak to me about the passion of her Son, and how much He loved me and wanted me to be with Him. My heart was gashed. She looked at me so kindly, and that look pierced my very soul. I was speechless, but at that moment I knew the response of love in my heart. I walked back down the hallway, through the door, and started my journey along the dirt path.

And in the morning, I awoke back in the dawn-lit tomb.

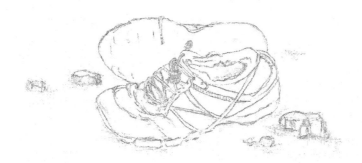

Prayer is the first rays of morning after a sleepless night. It is soothing and calm. It gives comfort and understanding. It has shed itself to find another. It is the first sign of victory in our hearts.

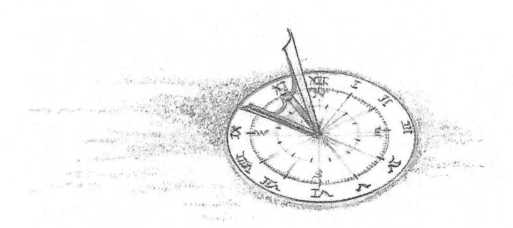

We have come to the last chapter in our journey. Over the past three chapters, we have focused on finding God in the midst of darkness, doubt, and suffering. Now we will try to part the storm clouds and see the rays of God's love coming through to us again, as they will at the end of our lives. We will end with an examination of the depth and breadth of God's love for us, and what it means for our hope. Jesus' death was not the end but the beginning, and so the same will be true for us at our death.

The Gospel of Matthew's account of the Resurrection states that the women who went to His burial place, after listening in amazement to the angels[76],

> went away quickly from the tomb, fearful yet overjoyed, and ran to announce this to his disciples. And behold, Jesus met them on their way and greeted them. They approached, embraced his feet, and did him homage. Then Jesus said to them, "Do not be afraid. Go tell my brothers to go to Galilee, and there they will see me."

We long to see Him, to obtain complete union with Him – a total self-giving, yes, but also a reception of what He has to offer. We are made to do both, and we are called to participate in the mystery of Divine Love. To this end, we have only our openness to offer Him, yet He offers us everything – His very self. The whole point of our spiritual life is to come to the climax of full and eternal union with God. It is the center of our prayers and actions. God will bring us to this moment when we are ready. For our part, we must continue to be as open as we can to His presence in every aspect of our lives.

It is not our love for God that will change us, but it is God's love for us that will do so. Consider how God spoke through His prophet Hosea[77], "I will betroth you to me forever: I will betroth you to me with justice and with judgment, with loyalty and with compassion; I will betroth you to me with fidelity, and you shall know the Lord." It is His love that will draw us out of ourselves

---

[76] Mathew 28:8-10
[77] Hosea 2:21-25

and heal our wounds. What is love? It is the very gift of self to the other. Imagine! God offers His whole, undivided self to you. He is inviting you, opening His arms to you, and saying[78], "All that I have is yours." Everything that He has is being poured out to you in His love. Know that He loves you deeply, and allow this truth to reach the depths of your heart, just as the morning rays pierce the darkness to reach the earth.

At every moment in our lives we seek to unite our whole selves to Christ because we love Him, and we love Him precisely because He loves us so much. That is why we desire to spend time with Him in the quiet of our hearts and to bring His peace to others. His love draws us in, transforming us, and giving us joy. In our responsiveness to His love, we find the freedom to enter into that loving union with all Being. One of the best ways to respond to His love is through our prayer where we take time to connect with Him.

Contemplation is not an attempt to wrap our minds around a mystery, but to simply be present to it with an open and listening heart. As we deepen our understanding of ourselves and of God we find our spiritual life becoming simpler and clearer. At bottom, our spiritual lives can be summarized in two truths. First, that God is love, and second, that we need to trust in His love in order to find our hearts desire, which is union with Him. These two truths are a refinement of everything else, and everything else finds its foundation here. Everything in our spiritual life follows from this: God loves us, and we ought to have total faith in His love.

Recall the words in the first letter of Peter[79], "Cast all your worries upon him because he cares for you." Be free to let your anxieties and concerns vanish in the presence of God. Hand them over to Him, and they will become lighter than air. Be at rest. Soak in His peace, and do not allow this passing world to disturb you. Each day is an opportunity to bring the light of God into the world. We can begin anew each day – the fresh wind of His love

---

[78] Luke 15:31
[79] 1 Peter 5:7

stirring in our hearts. Recall how the Holy Spirit entered the lives of the apostles[80], "suddenly there came from the sky a noise like a strong driving wind, and it filled the entire house in which they were. Then there appeared to them tongues as of fire, which parted and came to rest on each one of them."

To have God's presence in our souls is all we really need. As long as we are open to His presence in our souls, then we can be assured that He is doing the work that is necessary in our lives. He is sustaining our spirits, He is keeping everything in proper balance, and He is keeping our souls at peace. As the psalmist states[81], "Even though I walk through the valley of the shadow of death, I will fear no evil, for you are with me; your rod and your staff comfort me." That is why we need to spend time with Him in silence throughout our days, trusting that He will guide us safely home. It is this being-with-Him that provides us with hope in the mystery of His love.

Our hope then becomes like a nightlight which shines through the darkness and reminds us of the coming dawn. Its source is our prayer, which is like the electricity that keeps it lit. It keeps us in the heart of God our Heavenly Father, who will never lead us astray, but will always carry us in ways that are right and true. We have faith in His goodness because He has shown His love for us. Let us remember John's vision in Revelation[82],

> I heard a loud voice from the throne saying, "Behold, God's dwelling is with the human race. He will dwell with them and they will be his people and God himself will always be with them as their God. He will wipe every tear from their eyes, and there shall be no more death or mourning, wailing or pain, for the old order has passed away." The one who sat on the throne said, "Behold, I make all things new."

---

[80] Acts 2:2
[81] Psalm 23:4
[82] Revelation 21:3-5

Therefore, we can walk on though we do not know the way, for we know who leads us, and we know our destination.

✳✳✳

Wake the Sun

"Have you ever heard of the hermit who makes the sunrise?" they asked me. When I told them that I hadn't, they brought me to meet him, and I spent the night there talking with him. Late into the night he said, "We must first wake the birds." So, we went around the forest waking all the birds. Then we had to tell the stars to wake the sun. Next, the old hermit pulled out a long pipe, and as the smoke rose, it became beautifully colored clouds streaked across the sky. "Lastly," he said, "we must invite the sun to dance with the moon." He pulled out a harp and began playing and chanting a most wonderful song with the birds.

I sat on the hillside, watching and listening to this symphony of praise. As the first ray of sun flashed from over the edge of the earth, it pierced my heart with a glimpse of the New Creation. But just as quickly it fled, and I was left in its wake, entranced by the beauty of the sunrise.

At last, the old hermit stopped playing as the colors of the sunrise faded away and day fell into full swing. I decided to ask him if I could come again that night. He said it would be alright, so

I came again and got the same fleeting glimpse of the New Creation. I continued to come back night after night.

Finally, the old hermit said to me, "You will never fully understand nor find what you truly seek here. You must die and rise again, and I cannot help you with that. Go! God is calling you!"

Made in the USA
Columbia, SC
22 November 2017